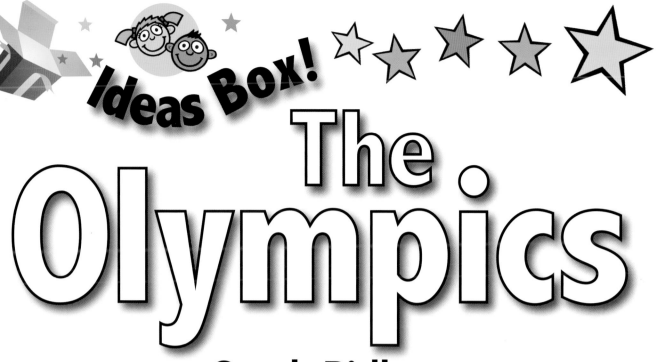

# Ideas Box!

# The Olympics

## Sarah Ridley

*A bit more practice and we could win Gold!*

W
FRANKLIN WATTS
LONDON • SYDNEY

espresso
education

First published in 2011 by
Franklin Watts
338 Euston Road
London NW1 3BH

Franklin Watts Australia
Level 17/207 Kent Street
Sydney NSW 2000

A CIP catalogue record for this book is
available from the British Library.

ISBN: 978 1 4451 0393 8
Dewey: 796.4'8

Series Editor: Sarah Peutrill
Art Director: Jonathan Hair
Series Designer: Matthew Lilly
Picture Researcher: Diana Morris
Illustrations by Artful Doodlers Ltd.

Printed in China

Franklin Watts is a division of
Hachette Children's Books,
an Hachette UK company
www.hachette.co.uk

Picture credits:
AFP/Getty Images: 21.
Diego Azubel/epa/Corbis: 1, 25t. Gero
Breloev/epa/Corbis: 16t. Andy
Clark/Reuters/Corbis: 19t. Phil Cole/Getty
Images: 20t. Michael Dalder/Reuters/
Corbis: 18b. Gallo Images/Getty Images:
27t. Kasa.dome/Shutterstock: 8c. Denis
Kornllov/Shutterstock: 7l. Reix-Liewig/
Corbis: front cover, 17bl. Mary416/
Shutterstock: 23t. Clive Mason/Getty
Images: 15b. Metropolitan Museum, New
York/Topfoto: 8b. Pete Niesen/
Shutterstock: 10b, 26b. Photonica/Getty
Images: 24b. Picturepoint/Topham: 10t.
Styve Reinecki/Shutterstock: 9b. Rex
Features: 5t. Hussain Sadequi/
Shutterstock: 7r. Jewel Samad/AFP/Getty
Images: 5b. Ullsteinbild/Topfoto: 14l.
Every attempt has been made to clear
copyright. Should there be any
inadvertent omission please apply to the
publisher for rectification.

# Contents

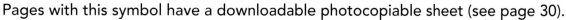

The Espresso friends:

I'm Sal and I'm 10.

I'm Ash and I'm 8.

I'm Scully and I'm Ash's dog.

I'm Kim and I'm 7.

I'm Polly and I'm 6.

I'm Scrap and I live with Polly and Eddy.

I'm Polly's brother, Eddy, and I'm 3.

Pages with this symbol have a downloadable photocopiable sheet (see page 30).

# The Olympic Games

Sal, Kim, Ash and Polly are looking forward to sports day at school. They really enjoy taking part in the activities. At the end of the afternoon there will be races between children of the same age. Everyone gets very excited, especially Eddy who cheers them all on. Sal hopes she will win the girls' running race like last year.

*All athletes should warm up properly!*

A new stadium and other buildings are created for each Olympic Games.

The friends wonder what it must be like to compete in the Olympic Games. Kim has been learning about the Olympics. He knows that they are held every four years in different cities around the world.

There are Summer and Winter Olympics, Paralympics and Youth Olympics. During the Summer Olympics, events take place over about 16 days with big opening and closing ceremonies attended by all the countries involved.

The Olympic Games begin with a dazzling opening ceremony. An athlete from each country parades their flag in the main stadium.

**?**

**Feedback...**

What is your favourite Olympic sport? Why?

# The ancient Olympics

Sal has been finding out about ancient Greece and the Olympic Games. They started in Greece about 2,800 years ago. Sal wrote a report for school.

## The Sporting Greeks

The Olympic Games were held to honour the Greek god, Zeus. They were the most important of the ancient Greek athletic festivals and took place every four years. They were held at Olympia, on the west coast of Greece, the site of a temple to Zeus.

In the early days, there was a one-day festival with a running race for young men. This developed into a five-day event including running, discus, wrestling, javelin and long jump competitions. The winners won an olive wreath, had a poem written about them and became famous.

At this time Greece was divided into many city-states. Two of the most important city-states were Athens and Sparta, who were often at war with each other. To prepare for war, boys and young men took regular exercise. Many of the sports they practised were good training for warfare. The best athletes entered the Olympics.

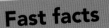

- The first recorded Olympics took place in 776 BC.
- The athletes competed naked.
- Only men and boys competed at the Olympics.
- The best athletes trained for ten months of the year.
- Emperor Theodosius abolished the Olympics in AD 393.

Olympia became buried under earth but was rediscovered in 1766.

*I'm glad that athletes wear clothes at the modern Olympics.*

This ancient statue shows an athlete throwing the discus, which is still an Olympic event.

# Events at the ancient Olympics

As the five-day festival was held in honour of the Greek god Zeus, the sports took place alongside processions, prayers and animal sacrifices. Kim decided to write a postcard to Ash, as if he had just watched the second day of the Olympics.

Dear Ash
Yesterday we watched the opening ceremony and the contests for boys. This morning we visited the Temple of Zeus and saw the huge statue inside. Then we all watched the chariot races and horse races. Two of the chariots crashed right in front of us! In the afternoon we saw the pentathlon — that's discus, javelin, long jump, running and wrestling competitions.
See you soon!
Kim

Zeus

This ancient Greek vase shows athletes running a race.

Thousands of spectators watched the Olympic Games. On the third day they saw running races – two sprints and a long-distance race. Wrestling, boxing and the penkration, a mixture of the two, entertained visitors on the fourth day. On the fifth and final day, the winners of the events took part in a procession to the Temple of Zeus. That completed the Olympics for another four years and everyone went home.

**Quiz:** What did athletes win at the ancient Olympics?

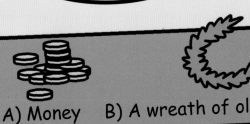

A) Money    B) A wreath of olive branches    C) A horse

Quiz answers are on page 32.

Starting blocks

This is the stadium at Olympia. The runners placed their feet in grooves cut into the stone slabs.

# The modern Olympics

Sal and Kim want to find out about the modern Olympic Games. It was Frenchman Baron Pierre de Coubertin who worked with a group of people to organise the first games in 1896. Held in Athens, Greece, they were a huge success.

The Panathenian Stadium in Athens was built for the first modern games in 1896.

Sal was surprised to discover that women were not allowed to take part in the Athens Olympics of 1896. Gradually this has changed. In London in 2012 women will compete in boxing, the last male-only Olympic sport.

Taking part in the Olympics remains the highest aim for many athletes.

**Swifter** **Higher** **Stronger**

The main aims of the modern Olympics are to bring people together in peace to celebrate sport and to encourage sport in education. The Olympic motto is: 'Citius, Altius, Fortius'. Translated from Latin this means 'Swifter, Higher, Stronger'.

## History spot: war and peace

In ancient Greece, the city-states agreed to a month of peace so that everyone could reach the Olympics safely. It was called the Olympic Truce. The Games were cancelled in 1916 due to the First World War (1914–18), and in 1940 and 1944 due to the Second World War (1939–45). One of the aims of the International Olympic Committee is to spread peace and understanding between countries through the Olympic Games.

**Quiz:**
Where will the next Olympic Games take place?

A) London, UK

B) Rio, Brazil

C) Singapore

# Design an Olympic kit

Each team of athletes from the same country wears special clothes for the Olympics. Sal has already designed a team kit. Here is her advice on how to get started.

**1** Look at photos for ideas. Some team kits display the national flag, or use the colours of the flag. You might want to use some Olympic symbols (see Art spot).

**2** Remember these clothes are for athletes. They MUST allow the athlete to perform at his or her best. They MUST be cool and comfortable. They MUST look good as the Olympics are watched by millions of people.

**3** Do you want to design a running kit, or come up with ideas for the whole team?

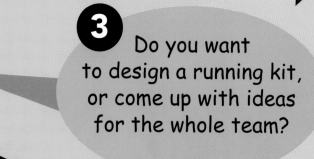

**4** Start drawing. Get several sheets of paper and sketch away.

**5** Find out about fabrics. Cotton is a cool, natural fabric but some fabrics keep the body at the correct temperature or help athletes to perform at their best.

## Art spot: symbols

In paintings, artists often use symbols to show ideas. The main Olympic symbols have been used on posters for the Olympics.

**Olympic rings:** these represent the five continents from which the athletes have travelled.

**Olive wreath:** a prize awarded to winners in ancient Greece.

**Dove:** represents peace.

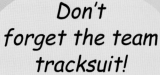

**Olympic flame:** this burns throughout the Olympics.

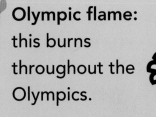

*Don't forget the team tracksuit!*

# All about the events

In 1896, 245 athletes took part in the Olympic Games. Today, around 10,000 athletes compete. There are 26 sports in the Summer Olympics. A sport has to be played around the world and approved by the International Olympic Committee to become an Olympic sport.

Kim enjoys watching the gymnastics most of all. There are so many events to choose from. The women's contests often include gym routines performed to music, using hoops, ribbons and ropes. The men compete for the best marks as they perform exercises on six pieces of gym equipment: the floor, horizontal bar, vault, parallel bars, pommel horse and rings.

*If I keep training, maybe I'll be in the Olympics one day.*

A gymnast uses great strength and balance when he performs on the rings.

Canoeing is great fun!

People sometimes forget about Olympic sailing, rowing, kayak and canoe contests. These usually take place away from the main stadium out at sea, or on a river or area of open water. Some of the canoe and kayak events are races on still water.

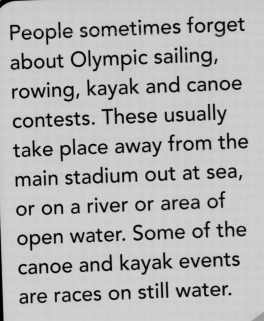

These Olympic sailors are using teamwork, fitness and skill to sail their boats to the finishing line.

GER

AUT

**Feedback...**

Which Olympic sport would you like to compete in? Why?

# Track and field

Some track and field events date back to the ancient Olympics. Today field events include the long jump, high jump and pole vault as well as throwing the javelin, discus and shot put. The track events can be some of the most exciting ones to watch, especially the sprints when athletes speed down the track as fast as their legs can go.

Pole vaulting

## PE spot: Olympics day

Kim and Ash organised their own Olympics day. It was hard work but great fun. Here is some of their advice.

Think ahead and get the teachers interested.

Draw up fair teams – for example a few children from each class. Select a range of events to allow school sports stars to shine as well as events that will involve everyone.

Olympics
on Thursday!!

Make posters, medals and certificates.

Invite spectators (your mums and dads) and don't forget to organise water stops. Enjoy!

Ash wrote a report for his newspaper about a famous sprinter.

Our reporter, Ash, investigates...

# LIGHTNING BOLT!

Superstar runner, Usain Bolt, is the fastest man on the planet. At the 2008 Olympics he made two new Olympic and world records and won three gold medals. He has broken the world records again since then. The Jamaican's performance continues to amaze the crowds.

## How does he run so fast?

Many would like to know the answer to that question. He has a long stride, he trains hard and he works on every last detail. For Bolt that means improving the race start, running the bends as fast as possible, improving fitness and being prepared.

By Ash

# The Winter Olympics

Ash, Kim and Eddy enjoy playing in the snow. They also love watching the Winter Olympics on television. Some of the events have really strange names, like the luge, a fast, dangerous toboggan race. Their favourite event is ski jumping.

A ski jumper takes off into the air, trying to make the longest jump possible.

The Winter Olympics started in 1924. They take place every four years, midway between one Summer Olympics and the next. There are seven sports – skiing, skating, bobsleigh, luge, ice hockey, curling and biathlon.

Curling is a team game. The aim is to slide heavy curling stones along the ice rink and into a target zone.

Many of the events take place at great speed down snowy mountains. Some of the athletes compete in curling and ice hockey matches held indoors.

## Quiz:
In the Winter Olympics, what is the biathlon?

A) A two-person long distance event

B) A cross-country skiing and shooting event

C) A 2-kilometre cross-country race

## Science spot: friction

Friction is the force between two surfaces that are moving across each other, or trying to move across each other. Friction always slows a moving object down. How quickly something slows down depends on the materials involved. A bobsleigh has blunt runners made of smooth steel to reduce friction. What other equipment used in winter sports tries to reduce friction to move faster?

### Feedback...
Which is your favourite Winter Olympic sport? Why?

# The Paralympics

The Paralympics take place straight after the Summer and Winter Olympics. All the competitors have a disability. There are events for wheelchair athletes, for athletes who use prosthetic limbs and for those who cannot see clearly.

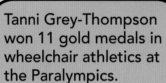
Tanni Grey-Thompson won 11 gold medals in wheelchair athletics at the Paralympics.

Ash has written a biography of a famous Paralympian.

Oscar Pistorius

Paralympic gold medallist and world record holder Oscar Pistorius was born in South Africa in 1986. At birth, he was missing some bones in his lower legs. Doctors decided to amputate below the knee and he was fitted with artificial, or prosthetic, legs.

Oscar went to school and played school sports. While recovering from a rugby injury in 2004 he discovered running. That same year he won a gold and a bronze medal at the Paralympics. In the 2008 Paralympics he won three more gold medals.

Oscar's springy prosthetic limbs have given him the nickname 'Blade Runner'. He runs so fast that he wants to compete against able-bodied athletes. After a big row over whether his blades give him an advantage in races, he is allowed to compete in all races. His dream is to run fast enough to compete in both the Olympics and the Paralympics.

## Fast facts

- In 1948 a wheelchair sports competition was held for soldiers injured in the Second World War.
- In 1960 the first Paralympics were held in Rome, Italy.
- The 'Para' in Paralympics comes from the Greek word 'beside' or 'alongside'.

 A spring

# Science spot: springs

A spring is material that holds a store of energy. Energy is the power to do work or make things happen. When Oscar Pistorius (above) runs on his prosthetic legs the springs in them release energy – and this is one of the reasons the Olympic officials felt that he had an unfair advantage.

# Games around the world

Ash and Kim wondered why the Olympics are held in a different city each time. They found out that the International Olympic Committee decides who will hold the next games. The chosen city, called the host city, and its country have about seven years to prepare for the Games.

The Olympics have been held in some countries more than once. Germany has held the Summer Olympics three times and the USA four times. Great Britain was awarded them for 1908, 1948 and 2012.

The National Stadium, or 'Bird's Nest', was the main stadium built for the 2008 Beijing Olympics.

The people who are organising the Olympics plan where to build the Olympic stadium, the swimming centre and all the other buildings needed for the events. Sometimes families have to move from their homes to make way for the Olympic buildings.

## Geography spot: Brazil

Rio de Janeiro in Brazil will host the Olympic Games in 2016. It will be the first time that the Olympics will take place in South America. Find out about Rio de Janeiro and Brazil. How many people live there? Which countries are its neighbours?

## Quiz:
The Olympic rings represent the continents where the athletes come from. There are only five rings. Which continent is not represented by a ring?

A) Antarctica

B) Africa

C) Asia

# What makes an Olympic champion?

Sal, Kim, Ash and Polly all play sport outside school. Sal has recently joined a running club and she trains twice a week. She decided to find out what makes an Olympic athlete.

Warming up stretches the muscles and prepares the body for action.

Most athletes who reach the Olympics discovered they were good at sport as children. They joined a club and trained for hours every week. They had to fit their training around their school or college work. That takes good planning as many athletes train for between four and six hours a day, most days of the week.

As training takes up so much time, young athletes have to really want to improve. They will not have as much time to see their friends or to relax. They will have to watch what they eat and make sure they get enough sleep. But when they win a race or competition it feels fantastic!

Tom Daley, Olympic diver, was 14 at the 2008 Olympics. He trains for four hours a day, six days a week.

*I love to eat beans on toast.*

## PSHE spot: a balanced diet

Like everyone, athletes need to eat a balanced diet with the right amounts of each food group. Because they take so much exercise, athletes need to eat more starchy foods, called carbohydrates, than usual. This food group includes pasta, rice, bread and cereals. In fact Polly's favourite meal of beans on toast is a healthy meal for athletes.

# Medals and world records

At sports day, Sal, Kim, Ash and Polly win points for their teams. At the Olympic Games athletes compete to win medals – a gold medal for first place, silver for second and bronze for third.

## Maths spot: medals data

During the Olympics, countries compete to win the maximum number of medals across all the events. Draw up an Olympic medal chart, collecting data from the official Olympics website. Decide what information to show. The chart could compare the number of medals won by each country or show the medals won by one country across various events. Think how to show the data clearly using colours, pictograms or numbers.

Olympic medallists stand on a podium to receive their medals.

Athletes also hope to become Olympic record-breakers. Officials at the Olympics keep careful records of the winners and details about their win. When an athlete breaks an Olympic record, the crowd goes wild. An Olympic record can only be broken at the Olympics. However the world record can be broken at any competition, including the Olympics. In 2008, Usain Bolt broke the Olympic and world records when he won the 100 and 200 metre sprints.

Kevin Paul of South Africa celebrates after breaking the Olympic and world records and winning gold at the 2008 Paralympics.

*Wow, maybe if I train hard, I could be a record breaker one day!*

# Make an Olympics board game

Kim and Ash have made a board game using what they have learnt about the Olympics. Polly wants to play it too. You could make your own board game.

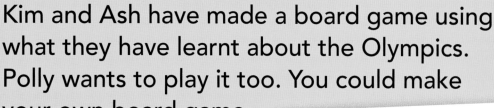

**1** Think about how your board game will look. Kim and Ash have made theirs like a running track but yours could be like another race. Think about the swimming or marathon events, for instance.

**2** Next think about the instructions. Make up at least 14. Look back through this book for ideas. Decide on the rules. How many times do you have to go round the board before you pass the 'winning line'?

Win gold!
Go on
3 places.

Pull a
muscle.
Go back 3
places.

**3** Take it in turns to roll the dice and move the counters around the board.

**4** Follow the instructions on the squares you land on.

Get cramp. Go back 1 place.

Break the Olympic record. Go on 5 places.

Trip over. Go back 3 places.

## Getting sporty
Your game instructions could include challenges to get all the players moving such as, 'Do 10 star jumps, then move forward three places'.

False start. Go back 1 place.

Win your heat. Go on 2 places.

Winning line

Start

# Glossary

**able-bodied athlete** An athlete who does not have a disability, as compared to a wheelchair athlete.

**animal sacrifice** To kill an animal as a gift for a god or goddess.

**athletics** Competitive sports including running, jumping and throwing events.

**balanced diet** Eating the right amount of all the types of food that the body needs.

**biathlon** A Winter Olympics sport which combines shooting and cross-country skiing.

**ceremony** A special event.

**city-state** In ancient Greece, a city and the land around it, with its own government, laws and army.

**continents** The six large land areas that make up the world.

**discus** A heavy round disc of wood, metal or stone.

**International Olympic Committee** The group of people who organise all the Olympic events.

**javelin** A light spear.

**olive wreath** Branches of the olive tree woven into a circle.

**Olympic flame** A symbol of the Olympic Games. It is lit in Olympia, Greece, and carried as a torch to the Olympic Games, to burn throughout the event.

**pole vault** A sport using a long springy pole to carry the athlete over a high bar.

**procession** A group of people moving forward in an organised way.

**prosthetic limb** An artificial limb used to replace a missing one.

**runners** On a bobsleigh, the two long pieces of metal that support the body of the bobsleigh.

**spectator** Someone who is watching an event.

**stadium** A large building for open-air sport.

**symbol** A sign or picture used to represent something.

**temple** A place of worship.

**toboggan** A type of sled.

**world record** The best ever performance for a particular sporting event.

**Youth Olympics** The Olympic event for 14- to 18-year-old athletes, first held in 2010 in Singapore.

**Zeus** King of the ancient Greek gods.

 Activity sheets

Go to www.franklinwatts.co.uk/downloads for free activity sheets.
Page 12: Download a fashion template to help you design your sports clothes.
Page 26: Download a worksheet for the medals table.

# Espresso connections

Here are a few ideas for how to take the contents of this book further using espresso. There are many more resources on the Olympics listed in the staffroom area under 'Resource Boxes'.

## Ancient Olympics/Ancient Greece (pages 4–9)

Find out more about ancient Greece and the Olympics in *History 2*, including information on Sparta, Athens and the gods. Go to the *News archive* in History and visit the *Ancient Greece* section for a video showing a Games Re-enactment.

## The modern Olympics (pages 10–11)

Find out more about the Olympic sports with videos and ideas in the *News 2 archive, PE, Olympics*. Visit the *Olympics Resource box* and select the *History* section and then *Olympic symbols* to explore the dove of peace and the IOC pledge to spread peace between nations through the Olympic Games.

## Design an Olympic kit (pages 12–13)

For photos and videos of past Olympic kits, look in the *News 2 archive > Olympics* under *PE*. Posters for the 1896 and 1948 Olympics can be found in the *Picture Gallery* in the *Olympics Resource Box*. Top tips for art techniques are in *Art 2*.

## Track and field (pages 16–17)

For help with an Olympics Day, go to *PE > News archive > Athletics and Olympics > More* and read the Espresso Extra 'Olympics at Strawberry Fields School' as well as *PE 2 > Athletics*.

## The Winter Olympics (pages 18–19)

Look at the *Olympics Resource box* in *PE 2, Vancouver 2010* and the *News archive* in *News 2 > PE* for stories about a Paralympic skier and more.

## The Paralympics (pages 20–21)

Look at the articles in *PE News archive > Olympics > Paralympics*. Also in the *Olympics Resource box*, under *Taking part* watch the video about an artificial low knee joint. Write a newspaper report about the achievements of Tanni Grey-Thompson, 11-times gold medallist.

## Games around the world (pages 22–23)

Sort the Olympic countries by putting them on the correct continents in *PE 2 > Olympics Resource box > Activity Arcade*. For news clips on London 2012, go to *PE 2 > News Archive > Olympics*.

## What makes an Olympic champion? (pages 24–25)

Find out about British Olympic champions in the *PE News Archive* and by watching interviews with Tom Daley in the *Olympics Resource Box* in *PE2*. *Team marathon* in *PE 2* contains useful resources, including a video.

## Medals and world records (pages 26–27)

For medal data, go to *Maths > News archive > Interpreting data* for examples of Olympic data. *Maths 2 > Premiership Football* helps with recording data in charts and tables.

# Index

## Quiz answers

Page 9: B) A wreath of olive branches
Page 11: London in 2012/Rio in 2016
Page 19: B) A cross-country skiing and shooting event
Page 23: A) Antarctica is not represented as no one lives there permanently

These are the lists of contents for each title in *Espresso Ideas Box!*:

## Chocolate

Where does chocolate come from? • How do cacao trees grow? • Cacao farming • The history of chocolate • Make a collage of the Aztec chocolate god • The chocolate trade • Make a chocolate piñata • Manufacturing chocolate • Is chocolate good for me? • Melting chocolate • Make chocolate leaves • Chocolate recipes • Chocolate heaven • Glossary and Activity sheets • Espresso connections

## Light

Light in the sky • Day and night • The Sun and seasons • Shadow play • Understanding eclipses • Light for life • Seeds and shoots • Rainbows • Make a rainbow spinner • Painting light • Turn the light on! • How do we see? • Holy light • Glossary and Activity sheets • Espresso connections

## Rainforests

What is a rainforest? • Rainforests around the world • Rainforest river • Life on the forest floor • Up in the trees • Play the music of the rainforest • Colourful rainforests • Animals in danger • Make a rainforest game • People of the rainorest • Disappearing rainforests • Save the rainforest • Have a rainforest debate • Glossary and Activity sheets • Espresso connections

## The Olympics

The Olympic Games • The ancient Olympics • Events at the ancient Olympics • The modern Olympics • Design an Olympic kit • All about the events • Track and field • The Winter Olympics • The Paralympics • Games around the world • What makes an Olympic champion? • Medals and world records • Make an Olympics board game • Glossary and Activity sheets • Espresso connections • Index and quiz answers

## Water

Water! • Solid, liquid, gas • The water cycle • Snow, hail and rain • Rivers • Floods • Painting water • Drinking water • Down the drain • Water and plants • Sacred water • Powerful water • Water for fun • Glossary and Activity sheets • Espresso connections

## Where you live

What is special about where you live? • Finding out about the past • What is the natural history of your area? • The square metre project • What can maps tell us? • Make a map stick • Changes to your area • Who lives in your area? • What jobs do people do? • Make a picture quiz • What problems are there in your area? • Famous connections • Attracting visitors to your area • Glossary and Activity sheets • Espresso connections